The Catholic Mother's Traditional Advent Journal

by

Mrs. Leane VanderPutten

Acknowledgements:

I would like to thank
my daughter-in-law,
Elizabeth VanderPutten,
for her expertise in editing this
book.
Her keen, critical eye was
invaluable to me.
I would also like to thank my family
for all their support,
advice and encouragement
along the way!

Foreword

Advent is such a special season! And you are about to make it more meaningful than you ever have!

This season of preparation is a wonderful time to impart to our children the importance of living the Liturgical year within our home. We go against the tide of what the world is telling us…through the glitz and the glitter, the hustle and bustle. We get our own captivating charm from the wonderful traditions and customs within our home that make the Birth of Christ something so much more than shopping, garland and tinsel.

All things in their proper time….according to Holy Mother Church! Jesus is not born yet! It is not Christmas but we are excitedly getting ready for the great celebration! Let's use this time to prepare our hearts for His coming, to show our children what living in the Church calendar means and how important it is!

I love this quote from Mary Reed Newland:

"For the families who begin to suspect that they have let their lives get too complicated with worldly cares, too much involved in secular values, too materialistic, living through the year with the Church is the stabilizer, the way to keep to first things first.

And for the families who conceal behind their front doors some hardship or cross, whether a suffering shared or inflicted or borne, the tempo of life in Christ as He leads the Church at prayer through the year is calming, enriching; it brings wisdom, sheds light, gives courage."

This Advent journal is for busy moms who need a little help making this season special within the home. It will help you stay on track and be consistent with the customs you have decided to incorporate within your four walls.

I have broken it down into bite-sized tidbits that, when laid out for you, will be easy to accomplish. As you check each item off you will get a sense of fulfillment knowing you are getting done what is truly important in this expectant season! The other things will get done….but first things first!

At midnight, on Christmas Eve, when Baby Jesus arrives, you and your family will look back upon your Advent and sigh with satisfaction, knowing you truly have celebrated with the Church, that you have put your best foot forward in making this a spiritual, enchanting, holy time for all!

The first few pages of this book will have a run-down of the special Advent customs and activities that will be on your checklist each day. They are simple, they are doable.

I hope this Advent is more special than ever as we walk hand-in-hand making the Liturgy come alive in our homes!
St. Nicholas, Pray for Us!
St. Lucy, Pray for Us!
Infant Jesus, King of Kings, Bless our Homes!

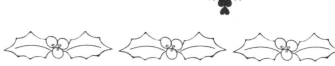

Customs, Activities & Prayers

Customs, Activities, Prayers

The Christmas Novena, The St. Andrew Novena

The Christmas Novena, the St. Andrew Novena (November 30th – December 24th), is one of the most popular Catholic Advent prayers.

Our Family says this novena each year in preparation for Christmas. We have family intentions that we offer up, and we also all have our own private intentions. It is always good to write these down so you can look at them periodically and so you can see how generous God has been in answering your prayers! Therefore, I will have a place for you to write down your intentions in this book.

In our family, we have found that we remember to say the Novena best when we say it after our daily Rosary. You could also say this novena with your grace before dinner while you light the candles as part of your Advent wreath prayers.

In this Advent season of preparing for Christ's coming, the St. Andrew Christmas Novena is a loving way to prepare ourselves and our families.

St Andrew holds the honor of being the first apostle to be called by Christ to follow Him.

This novena is a bit different in that it does not invoke the intervention or aid of the saint himself, but is adoring, glorifying the hour of Christ's birth and seeking aid from God Himself!

The novena is begun on the Feast of Saint Andrew, November 30th, and is said thru Christmas Eve, December 24th.

**(If you start late, or if you miss a day do not be discouraged! Catch up by saying the extra prayers you missed along the way....Jesus will bless every effort!)

ST. ANDREW CHRISTMAS NOVENA

Hail and Blessed be the hour and the moment in which the Son of God was born of the most pure Virgin, in Bethlehem, at midnight, in piercing cold.

In that hour, vouchsafe, O my God, to hear my prayer and grant my desires through the merits of Our Savior Jesus Christ and of His Blessed Mother. Amen.

Recite 15 times per day.

The Advent Wreath

The symbolism of the Advent wreath is beautiful.
The wreath is made of various evergreens which make us think of everlasting life.
The four candles represent the four weeks of Advent.
Three candles are purple and one is rose. The purple candles symbolize the prayer,
penance and preparatory sacrifices and goods works that we do at this time.
The rose candle is lit on the third Sunday, Gaudete Sunday, when the priest also wears
rose vestments at Mass; it is the Sunday of rejoicing, because the faithful have arrived
midway in Advent, and Christmas is getting closer....
In family practice, the Advent wreath can be lit at dinner time after the blessing of the
food.

Throughout the journal I will remind you each day to say the Advent
Wreath Prayers that are found on the following page.

Advent Wreath Prayers
The Beginning of Advent

[On the Saturday before the First Sunday of Advent, the family gathers around the wreath decorated with greens.
[One candle should be lit.]

ler: We gather around our wreath to begin the celebration of Advent. Let us ask our Father in heaven to fill our hearts with grace.
(Silent pause for prayer.)
.venly Father, we look forward to the celebration of Christmas and to the coming of the Lord in glory. Bless this Advent wreath and all of us. As we pray daily around it, fill us with Your life and strengthen us for our daily tasks. We ask this through Christ our Lord.
All: Amen.

The First Week of Advent [One candle is lit.]
der: Heavenly Father, as we begin this Advent, give light to our eyes and peace to our hearts. May the Lord find us watching and waiting in joy when He comes. We pray in Jesus' name.
All: Amen.

The Second Week of Advent [Two candles are lit.]
nder: Father in heaven, set our hearts ablaze to follow in the steps of John the Baptist. May we bring light and love to all we meet, that the darkness of sin and fear may be overcome. In Christ's name we ask this.
All: Amen.

The Third Week of Advent [Three candles are lit.]
nder: As we draw near to You, Lord God, keep us aware of Your presence in all we do. Come with power to enlighten us by your grace, that we may live in praise and peace all our days. We ask this through Christ our Lord.
All: Amen.

Special Days of Preparation
[Traditionally, the days from December 17 to the day before Christmas have as their focus the titles of Jesus. On these days, a special cripture passage may be read to recall these titles. Three candles are used until the Fourth Sunday of Advent, when all four candles are lit.]

December 17
Jesus, the Wisdom of God: 1 Cor 1:26-31
Leader: Come, O Wisdom of God Most High, and fill our hearts with Your word of truth.
All: Come Lord Jesus!

December 18
Jesus, the new Lawgiver: Mt. 17:1-8
Leader: Come, O Giver of the Law, that we may be strengthened by Your mighty power.
All: Come Lord Jesus!

December 19
Jesus, the Flower of Jesse: Rom. 15:7-13
Leader: Come, O Flower of Jesse's Root, that we may be made fruitful witnesses of Your love.
All: Come Lord Jesus!

December 20
Jesus, the Key of David Rev. 3:7-8
Leader: Come, O Key of David, to unlock the darkness of sin and free us by Your grace.
All: Come Lord Jesus!

December 21
Jesus, the Radiant Dawn Is. 9:1-6
Leader: Come, O Radiant Dawn, sun of justice, and fill us with Your saving light.
All: Come Lord Jesus!

December 22
Jesus, the King of the Nations Rev. 19:11-16
Leader: Come, O King of the Nations, and bind us all together in the unity and peace we seek.
All: Come Lord Jesus!

December 23
Jesus, Emmanuel Mt. 1:18-23
Leader: Come, O Emmanuel, presence of God among us, and fill our hearts with every good gift.
All: Come Lord Jesus!

December 24
[On Christmas Eve, the wreath can be renewed with new greenery and the candles replaced with new white tapers for use during the Christmas season.]
Leader: Lord Jesus, we approach that holy moment when Your coming as man is renewed in our hearts. Give us peace and allow us to lebrate Your presence with joy, that we may some day share Your glory. We ask this of You, who live and reign with the Father and the Holy Spirit, as One God, now and forever.
All: Amen.

The Christmas Season
[From Christmas Day until the Baptism of the Lord, the following prayer can be used with the wreath.]
ader: Father in heaven, You so loved us that You sent Your Son, among us as Savior and Lord. Fill us with Your blessing, that we may grow in love and continue to live our Christian faith. We ask this through Christ our Lord.
All: Amen.

The Blessing of a Christmas Tree

There are many legends and much symbolism behind the Christmas tree. The Christmas tree is a sign of the great Tree of the Cross; it is noble because it is by a tree that the whole world has been redeemed. The splendor of the Christmas tree reminds us of the redemption of even the material creation by Christ -- and recalls the lovely legend that all the trees on earth blossomed forth on Christmas night. And the evergreen is traditional for the Christmas tree, for it reminds us of the everlasting life that Christ won through His Incarnation, Death and Resurrection.

Some time in the evening the tree is blessed by the father of the family, and afterwards the festive lights are lit for the first time. The following form may be used for the blessing.

FATHER: O God, come to my assistance.

ALL: O Lord, make haste to help me. Glory be to the Father and to the Son and to the Holy Spirit. As it was in the beginning, is now and ever shall be, world without end. Amen.

FATHER: Then shall all the trees of the forest exult before the Lord, for He comes.

ALL: Sing to the Lord a new song; sing to the Lord, all you lands.

FATHER: Sing to the Lord; bless His name; announce His salvation day after day.

ALL: Tell His glory among the nations; among all peoples, His wondrous deeds.

FATHER: For great is the Lord and highly to be praised; awesome is He, beyond all gods.

ALL: Splendor and majesty go before Him; praise and grandeur are in His sanctuary.

FATHER: Give to the Lord, you families of nations, give to the Lord glory and praise; give to the Lord the glory due His name!

ALL: Bring gifts, and enter His courts; worship the Lord in holy attire.

FATHER: Tremble before Him, all the earth; say among the nations: the Lord is King.

ALL: Let the heavens be glad and the earth rejoice; let the sea and what fills it resound; let the plains be joyful and all that is in them!

FATHER: Then shall all the trees of the forest exult before the Lord, for He comes; for He comes to rule the earth.

ALL: He shall rule the world with justice and the peoples with his constancy.

FATHER: Glory be to the Father and to the Son and to the Holy Spirit.

ALL: As it was in the beginning, is now and ever shall be, world without end. Amen.

FATHER: Then shall all the trees of the forest exult before the Lord, for He comes.

MOTHER: Lesson from Isaias the Prophet. Thus saith the Lord: The land that was desolate and impassable shall be glad, and the wilderness shall rejoice and shall flourish like the lily. It shall bud forth and blossom, and shall rejoice with joy and praise: the glory of Libanus is given to it: the beauty of Carmel, and Saron, they shall see the glory of the Lord and the beauty of our God.

ALL: Thanks be to God.

FATHER: And there shall come forth a rod out of the root of Jesse

ALL: And a flower shall rise up out of His root.

FATHER: O Lord, hear my prayer.

ALL: And let my cry come to You.

FATHER: Let us pray. O God, who hast made this most holy night to shine forth with the brightness of the True Light, deign to bless this tree (sprinkles it with holy water) which we adorn with lights in honor of Him who has come to enlighten us who sit in darkness and in the shadow of death. And grant that we upon whom is poured the new light of Thy Word made flesh may show forth in our actions that which by faith shines in our minds. Through Christ our Lord.

ALL: Amen.

The Sacrifice Manger

This is a simple and wonderful little activity that encourages the children, in the Spirit of Advent, to deny themselves in order to prepare their hearts for the coming of Jesus at Christmas!

You can either use the manger that belongs to your Nativity Scene or you can do what we did through the years... We made a bigger one out of small twigs or popsicle sticks that we glued together.

For the straw, we cut paper into small strips and as the children did sacrifices, said extra prayers or did good deeds throughout the day, they could put a paper straw in the manger. Each child could have their own color of paper straw or they could just write their inital on the straw cut from regular white paper....just to personalize it a bit. You can also use real straw or hay, cut into pieces and, as the children do their sacrifices, they can watch as the manger slowly gets softer and softer, readying it for the Baby Jesus!

He wore His swaddling clothes as if they were Tyrian purple. He lay in a manger that seemed like a conquered world. He opened His tiny arms, and their circle was vast enough to embrace all humanity. He smiled, and the light of a new era dawned.
-Fr. Daniel A. Lord

The Stable

Your Nativity Scene is just that - YOUR Nativity Scene. Everyone will have their own unique scene depending on where you purchase the actual figurines, how much detail you go into when setting up the scenery around it, how many older children you have to help, how much time you have to spend on it, etc.

We try to get ours set up at the beginning of Advent, leaving out the Holy Family statues until the last week and then putting Baby Jesus in His manger (sneakily, to add to the thrill) so He is there after Midnight Mass (or in the morning before the children wake up, if you go to Mass on Christmas morn).

My Spiritual Christmas Crib

"Build your Spiritual Christmas Crib in your heart by these short day-by-day meditations and practices for December 1–24. It's a perfect activity to practice with your family!" – Sisters, Slaves of the Immaculate Heart of Mary

This is a custom we have kept throughout the years. It is a beautiful little devotion preparing our hearts for the coming of Our Lord at Christmas.

You can do the special activities indicated each day in this devotion in your own Manger Scene. When my older ones were young we made a 3D stable out of heavy cardboard and added the different themes each day…whether it was drawing in the cobwebs or making paper doll figurines for the Nativity Scene.

Or you can do what we have done the last few years. We put up 4 big white posterboard papers on an empty wall to make a big blank paper just waiting for the crayons and sharpies to make their mark! (You can make it as big or small as you like, using just one or two posterboards or even just a sheet of regular cardstock posted on the refrigerator.) Each morning we draw the part of the manger scene that is applicable to that day. In order to get ideas on how to draw some parts of the scene, we look for coloring pages on the internet for the Nativity Scene or for other parts of the stable we want to draw. The images are easy to sketch when taken from a children's coloring page!

One of my older daughters or I usually do the pencil drawing then one of the children traces it with colored markers and colors it in. It needn't be complicated….a quick drawing does the trick! We also print out (or write out) the special prayer for the day and put the assigned one up so we can say it throughout the day. This is not necessary if it is too time-consuming for a busy mother. Just repeat the little prayer a few times with the children when you first do the activity and they can try to remember it throughout the day.

This is a wonderful family devotion that helps to make Advent and Christmas meaningful!

I will post each day's devotion on your Advent Journal Page of the Day.

Below are pictures of what our Spiritual Christmas Crib has looked like at the end of the season. See? you don't have to be artists! :)

The Rosary

Although not a specific Advent custom, the daily Rosary will be included in your checklist each day. If you don't get anything else done from the list for that day, but you are able to put a checkmark by the Rosary, you have done the most important thing!

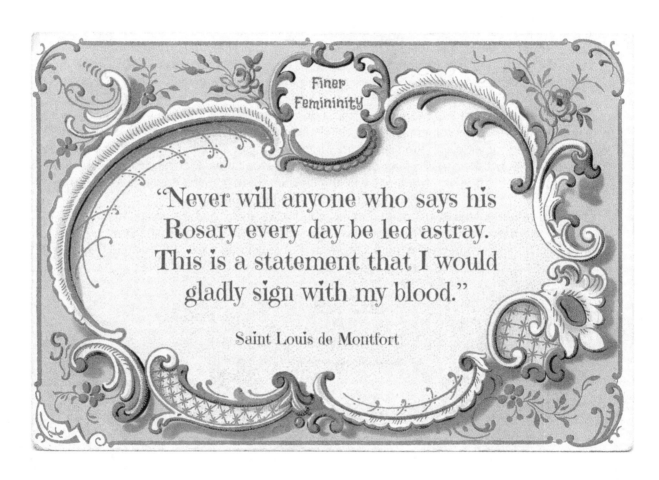

Finer Femininity

"Never will anyone who says his Rosary every day be led astray. This is a statement that I would gladly sign with my blood."

Saint Louis de Montfort

"The Rosary is a powerful weapon to put the demons to flight and to keep oneself from sin...If you desire peace in your hearts, in your homes, and in your country, assemble each evening to recite the Rosary. Let not even one day pass without saying it, no matter how burdened you may be with many cares and labors." – Pope Pius XI

"There is also the question of time.
Where do we find the time to participate in the **Church's liturgical year** with our children?
Like these other questions, the answer is, **we can find it if we plan for it.**
We can find it quite easily by looking to see where we waste it.
Not wasting it is not easy, because the habits of time-wasting, although they are harmless, are hard to break – as I know from experience.
Mothers have this struggle all to themselves. It involves such things as the radio (now internet) habit, coffee breaks, long telephone conversations, chatting with neighbors, a heavy involvement in outside activities.
Somewhere most American women CAN "find time" to devote to the **enriching of their families' spiritual life.**
The joyous discovery is that once we have struggled and found the time, **tasted and seen how sweet are these pursuits together,** we begin to gauge all our doings so that there will be time – because we are convinced **there must be."**
-Mary Reed Newland, The Year and Our Children

Your Advent Checklist & Planner

Your Checklist for the Last Week of November!

A Week before Advent you should start thinking about what you need for your Advent activities, buy the necessary materials or dig them up out of your Christmas storage. It is so much nicer, when that first Sunday of Advent hits (or December 1st - whichever comes first), and you have everything ready to start on time.

Once you gather each item up, put a checkmark in the star! ⭐

Advent Wreath (Buy one or make one)..............⭐

Candles (3 purple, 1 pink)...........................⭐

Nativity Scene...................................⭐
  (If you already have one, get it out. If you don't, invest in one, if you can.)

Posterboard......................................⭐
  (As big or little as you want... for the Spiritual Christmas Crib)

Sharpies & Crayons..............................⭐

Stockings (for St. Nicholas Day).......................⭐

Advent Calendar.................................⭐
  (Get out your old one or purchase one.)

Sacrifice Manger (Homemade or bought)...........⭐

Straw (Construction paper or real straw or hay)..........⭐

Holy Water (For the Blessing of the Christmas Tree).....⭐

St. Andrew Novena Petitions

If you have the faith of a mustard seed....
It is piously believed that whoever recites the St. Andrew Christmas Novena
prayer FIFTEEN times each day will obtain the favor requested.
Let us ask, let us believe! God is not wanting in generosity!
In the lines below write down your family petitions for this Novena.
Below that, write down your own private intentions.
It is a beautiful thing to look back and see how God has answered our
prayers, so writing them down is very efficacious!

Family Petitions

_____

_____

_____

_____

_____

_____

_____

_____

_____

Private Petitions

_____

_____

_____

_____

_____

_____

_____

_____

_____

The St. Andrew Novena/The Christmas Novena is found on page 3. The Novena is from Nov. 30th - Dec. 24th.

The beginning of Advent fluctuates. This journal (besides reminding you on this page to start the St. Andrew Novena on Nov. 30th) begins on December 1st.
If the First Sunday of Advent happens to come before Dec. 1st, start the Advent Wreath Prayers and the Sacrifice Manger on that day.
Then begin journaling on December 1st!
Happy Advent!!

November 30th ~ St. Andrew's Feast Day
Beginning of your St. Andrew Novena!
(found on page 3)

St. Andrew, pray for us!

Put a ✓ in the heart if you remembered to start your St. Andrew Novena (pg. 3) today. If you missed it, don't get discouraged, say it twice the next day!

3 Grateful Gifts for Today:
(So many blessings....take note!)

1. _____

2. _____

3. _____

1 Tiny Tidbit for Today:

(An inspiration, a kind word, a memorable visit with a friend, etc.)

Be a woman of hope, optimism and goodwill!

_____

_____

_____

Advent Quote:

Spiritual Christmas Crib

DEC.1 – THE STABLE

Frequently during the day offer your heart to the little Infant Jesus. Ask Him to make it His home.

Sweet Jesus, take my heart and make it meek and pure.

During Advent, the "spring-time" of the Church, we must arouse ourselves and bring forth new fruits of sanctity. If we have been somewhat drowsy and languid in Our Lord's service, now is the time to arouse ourselves to a new life, to strip ourselves generously of our meanness and weakness and to "put on Jesus Christ", that is, His holiness.

Divine Intimacy
Fr. Gabriel of St. Mary Magdalen, O.C.D.

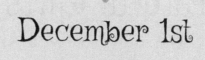

December 1st

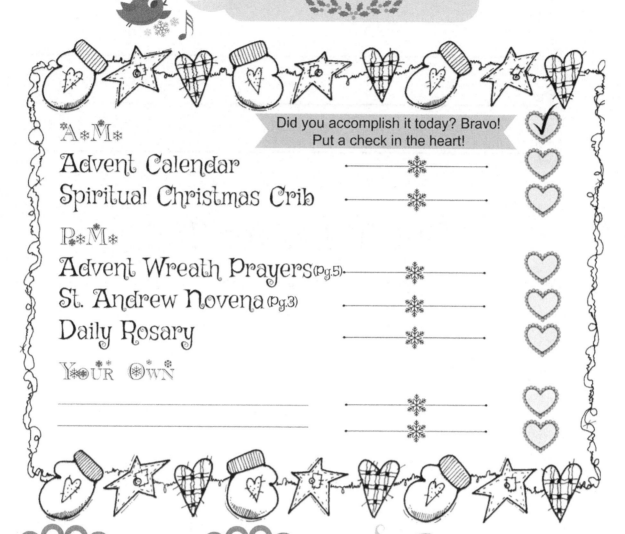

A*M*

Advent Calendar

Spiritual Christmas Crib

P*M*

Advent Wreath Prayers (pg.5)

St. Andrew Novena (pg.3)

Daily Rosary

Your Own

_____

_____

Did you accomplish it today? Bravo!
Put a check in the heart!

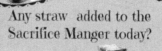

Any straw added to the Sacrifice Manger today?

Mothers, as Christmas closes in, know how very important you are. Your smile lightens the burdens, your words brighten the hearts of those who will be part of your festivities. The tone of this special family time is set by you! We, as mothers, are privileged to have such an important part in the making of our homes! May this Advent Season be filled with grace and love!

3 Grateful Gifts for Today:
(So many blessings....take note!)

1. _____

2. _____

3. _____

1 Tiny Tidbit for Today:

(An inspiration, a kind word, a memorable visit with a friend, etc.)

Having a happy home is crucial to the spreading of our faith.
-Fr. Lasance

_____

_____

_____

Spiritual Christmas Crib

DEC.2 – THE ROOF
See that the roof of the stable is in good condition, so that the Infant Jesus is protected from rain and snow. This you will do by carefully avoiding every uncharitable remark.

Jesus, teach me to love my neighbor as myself.

Advent Quote:

O Lord, I cannot doubt Your tenderness, because You have given me proofs of it in so many ways, with the sole purpose of convincing me of it. Therefore, trusting in Your love, my weak love will become strong with Your strength.
-Divine Intimacy
Fr. Gabriel of St. Mary Magdalen, O.C.D.

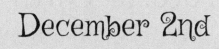

December 2nd

A·M·

Advent Calendar ——— ❄

Spiritual Christmas Crib ——— ❄

P·M·

Advent Wreath Prayers (pg.5) ——— ❄

St. Andrew Novena (pg.3) ——— ❄

Daily Rosary ——— ❄

Your Own

_____ ——— ❄

_____ ——— ❄

Did you accomplish it today? Bravo!
Put a check in the heart!

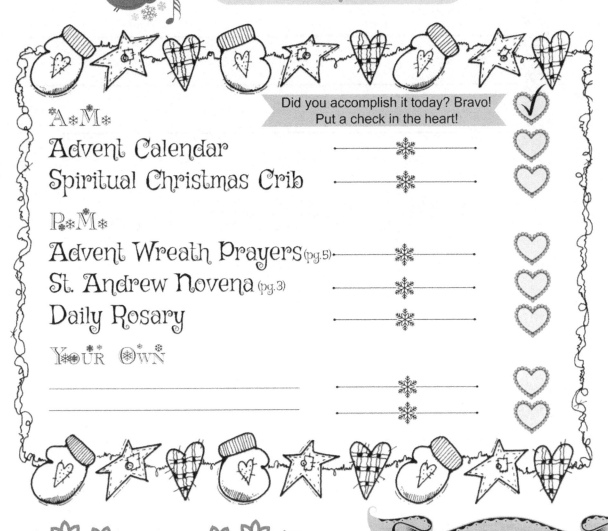

Let us not forget that in true womanliness is our strength, and that the end of our being is to comfort and bless and love...
Annie S. Swan,
The Gentle Art
of Homemaking,
1893

Any straw added to the
Sacrifice Manger today?

3 Grateful Gifts for Today:
(So many blessings....take note!)

1. _____
2. _____
3. _____

1 Tiny Tidbit for Today:

(An inspiration, a kind word, a memorable visit with a friend, etc.)

We are called to love, bless, and encourage those around us, especially in the home.

_____

_____

_____

Advent Quote:

Spiritual Christmas Crib

DEC.3 – CREVICES
Carefully stop every crevice in the walls of the stable, so that the wind and cold may not enter there. Guard your senses against temptations. Guard especially your ears against sinful conversations.

Jesus, help me to keep temptations out of my heart.

To whom do we want to spread our faith? First of all, to our children. They need to see the deep and lasting beauty of our faith shining forth in our everyday lives, making our home beautiful and happy. Our faith should be an unspoken reality, the undercurrent in the everyday bubbling brook, that flows into every facet of our lives, without it being brassy or aggressive.

–Leane VanderPutten

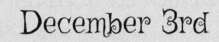

December 3rd

A∗M∗

Advent Calendar ⟶ ❄

Spiritual Christmas Crib ⟶ ❄

P∗M∗

Advent Wreath Prayers (pg.5) ⟶ ❄

St. Andrew Novena (pg.3) ⟶ ❄

Daily Rosary ⟶ ❄

Your Own

_____ ❄

_____ ❄

Did you accomplish it today? Bravo!
Put a check in the heart!

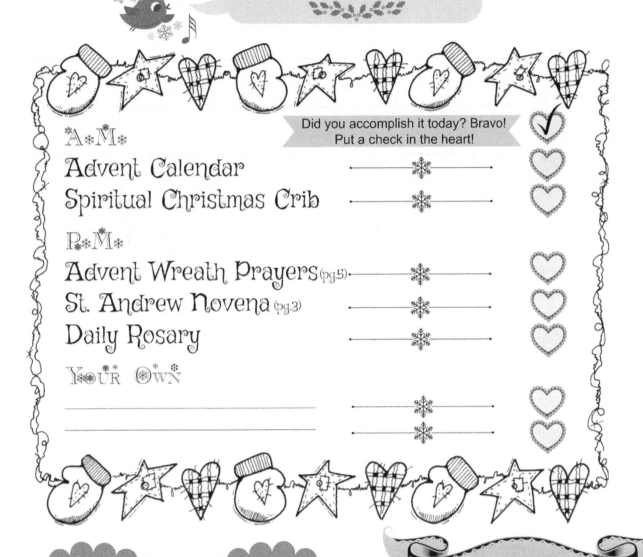

Any straw added to the
Sacrifice Manger today?

For years, while raising children, a mother's time is never her own, her own needs have to be kept in second place, and every time she turns around a hand is reaching out and demanding something. Hence, a mother raising children, perhaps in a more privileged way even than a professional contemplative, is forced, almost against her will, to constantly stretch her heart.
—Fr. Rolheiser, **OMI**

3 Grateful Gifts for Today:
(So many blessings....take note!)

1. _____
2. _____
3. _____

1 Tiny Tidbit for Today:

(An inspiration, a kind word, a memorable visit with a friend, etc.)

No matter how plain our home may be, nor how old-fashioned, if love and prayer be in it, it will be a transfigured spot.

_____

_____

_____

Advent Quote:

Spiritual Christmas Crib

DEC.4 – COBWEBS
Clean the cobwebs from your spiritual crib. Diligently remove from your heart every inordinate desire of being praised. Renew this intention at least three times today.

My Jesus, I want to please You in all I do today.

Far more than we know do the strength and beauty of our lives depend upon the home in which we dwell. He who goes forth in the morning from a happy, loving, prayerful home, into the world's strife, temptation, struggle, and duty, is strong — inspired for noble and victorious living.
-J.R. Miller

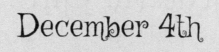

December 4th

Did you accomplish it today? Bravo!
Put a check in the heart!

A·M·

Advent Calendar

Spiritual Christmas Crib

P·M·

Advent Wreath Prayers (pg.5)

St. Andrew Novena (pg.3)

Daily Rosary

Your Own

_____

_____

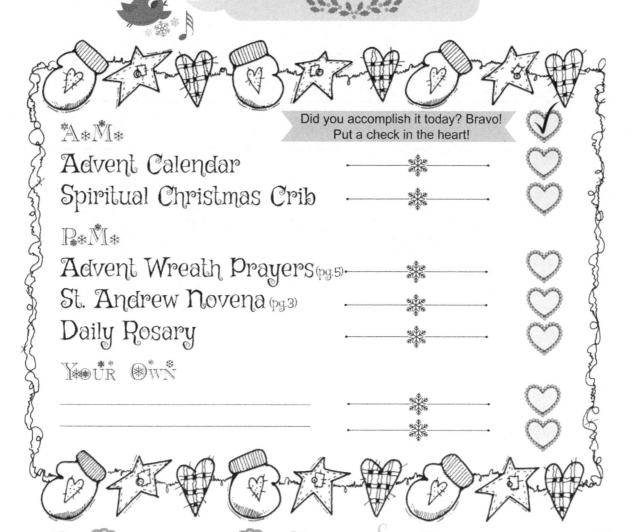

Any straw added to the Sacrifice Manger today?

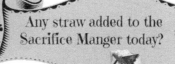

Be attentive to the sacrifices your husband makes for the family. Each day he battles the world, the flesh and the devil out in the workforce for you. Don't let that go unnoticed. Thank him often! Appreciate him.

3 Grateful Gifts for Today:
(So many blessings....take note!)

1. _____

2. _____

3. _____

1 Tiny Tidbit for Today:

(An inspiration, a kind word, a memorable visit with a friend, etc.)

Let us live more for our homes. Let us love one another more.

_____

_____

_____

Spiritual Christmas Crib

DEC.5 – FENCE
Build a fence about the crib of your heart by keeping a strict watch over your eyes, especially at prayer.

Sweet Jesus, I long to see You.

Advent Quote:

For Christmas begins and ends with a Child. About the Infant in the manger prophecies are fulfilled, and angels sing, and the poor kneel giftless save for the unpurchasable gift of patient affection, and the rich come gilt-laden, but with a strange humility bringing low their heads, and all mankind is reborn to a new era of grace and hope and God's revelation of love and graciousness.
-Rev. Daniel A. Lord

December 5th

A*M*

Advent Calendar

Spiritual Christmas Crib

P*M*

Advent Wreath Prayers (pg.5)

St. Andrew Novena (pg.3)

Daily Rosary

Your Own

_____

_____

Did you accomplish it today? Bravo! Put a check in the heart!

Today is the day to fill the stockings (or shoes) and tuck them away for the Feast of St. Nicholas tomorrow!

Any straw added to the Sacrifice Manger today?

3 Grateful Gifts for Today:
(So many blessings....take note!)

1. _____

2. _____

3. _____

1 Tiny Tidbit for Today:
(An inspiration, a kind word, a memorable visit with a friend, etc.)

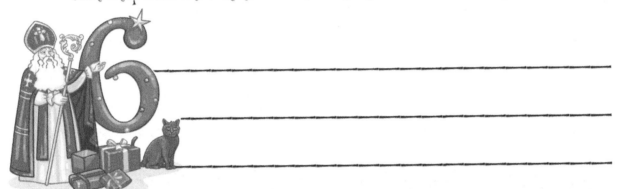

_____

_____

_____

Spiritual Christmas Crib

DEC. 6 – MANGER
Fix the best and warmest corner of your heart for the manger of Jesus. You will do so by abstaining from what you like most in the line of comfort and amusement.

Mary, use these sacrifices to prepare my heart for Jesus in Holy Communion.

Advent Quote:

Probably not all children who discover there is no Santa, when they have been told by their parents that there is, will consider their parents dyed-in-the-wool liars, but there is the danger that they will discount some of every other truth they are taught. This is an age when accuracy and unadorned truthfulness are not particularly in vogue. Yet a concern to speak the utter truth in everything will teach a child better than anything else how to be utterly truthful himself, how to be honest with his own conscience – which is the same thing as being honest with God. Santa Claus is not a serious lie, but St. Nicholas in his rightful place, gazing with us at the Christ Child, is a much lovelier truth.

Mary Reed Newland

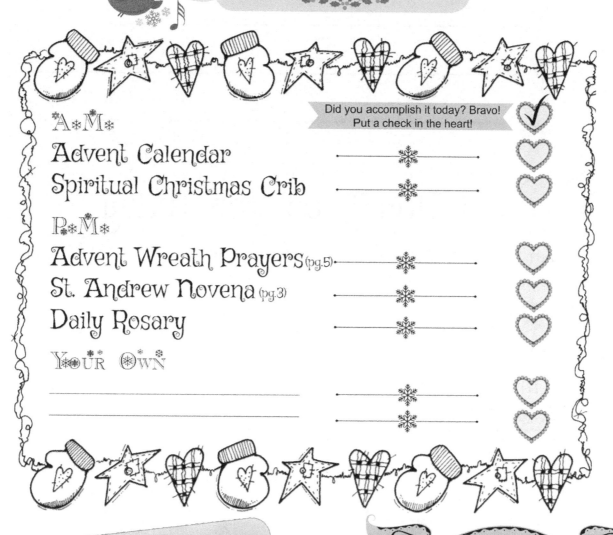

A·M·

Advent Calendar

Spiritual Christmas Crib

P·M·

Advent Wreath Prayers (pg.5)

St. Andrew Novena (pg.3)

Daily Rosary

Your Own

_____

_____

Did you accomplish it today? Bravo!
Put a check in the heart!

Do Something Special Today!
-Read the St. Nicholas Story
-Watch the St. Nicholas cartoon
-Color/Draw a picture of St. Nicholas
-Add a simple prayer to him at Rosary time
-Put on a simple Puppet Show
-Make a cake
Keep it Simple, Make it Special!

Any straw added to the Sacrifice Manger today?

Telling the truth about Santa Claus need not rob children of their Christmas magic. It adds to it with another feast to celebrate, another saint to know and love, another emphasis gently persuading them to meditate on the coming of the Divine Child.
-Mary Reed Newland

3 Grateful Gifts for Today:
(So many blessings....take note!)

1. _____
2. _____
3. _____

1 Tiny Tidbit for Today:

(An inspiration, a kind word, a memorable visit with a friend, etc.)

See the good in all things!

_____
_____
_____

Advent Quote:

Spiritual Christmas Crib

DEC. 7 – HAY
Supply the manger of your heart with hay, by overcoming all feelings of pride, anger or envy.

Jesus, teach me to know and correct my greatest sins.

If there is no Advent, then Christmas is not adequately experienced. If you do not experience the message of Advent and therefore do not look for Jesus to come, then do not be surprised that Christmas seems to slip by without leaving a mark on the soul.
-Gift of Faith

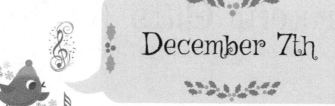

December 7th

*A*M*

Advent Calendar

Spiritual Christmas Crib

P*M*

Advent Wreath Prayers (pg.5)

St. Andrew Novena (pg.3)

Daily Rosary

Your Own

Did you accomplish it today? Bravo!
Put a check in the heart!

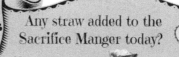

Any straw added to the
Sacrifice Manger today?

Cultivate kindness of heart; think well of your fellow-men; look with charity upon the shortcomings in their lives; do a good turn for them, as opportunity offers; and, finally, don't forget the kind word at the right time. How much such a word of kindness, encouragement, of appreciation means to others sometimes, and how little it costs us to give it!
- J.R. Miller

3 Grateful Gifts for Today:

(So many blessings....take note!)

1. _____

2. _____

3. _____

1 Tiny Tidbit for Today:

(An inspiration, a kind word, a memorable visit with a friend, etc.)

THE MEASURE OF LOVE
IS TO LOVE WITHOUT
MEASURE.
-St. Francis de Sales

_____

_____

_____

Advent Quote:

Spiritual Christmas Crib

DEC. 8 – SOFT STRAW

Provide your manger with soft straw by performing little acts of mortification; for instance, bear the cold without complaints; or sit and stand erect.

Dear Jesus, Who suffered so much for me, let me suffer for love of You.

God does not live in time. He invented time for us so that we could keep track of ourselves, but He has no need of it, and in the foreverness of Heaven, He used all the magnificent graces His Divine Son poured forth from His death on the Cross in time to merit for our Lady a perfect soul from the instant He breathed it into being.

That is why, when Gabriel came to her in Nazareth, he could say, "Hail, full of grace...." That is why, when Mary went to visit Elizabeth, Elizabeth could cry out, "Blessed art thou among women...."

-Mary Reed Newland, The Year and Our Children

December 8th
Happy Feast of the
Immaculate Conception!

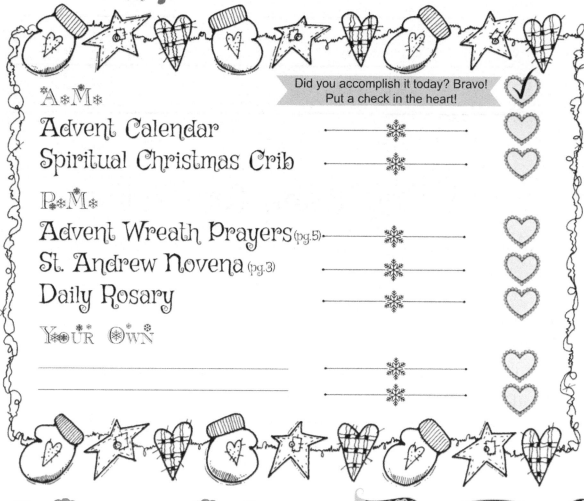

Did you accomplish it today? Bravo!
Put a check in the heart!

*A*M*

Advent Calendar

Spiritual Christmas Crib

*P*M*

Advent Wreath Prayers (pg.5)

St. Andrew Novena (pg.3)

Daily Rosary

Your Own

_____

_____

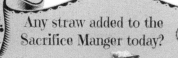

Any straw added to the
Sacrifice Manger today?

O Mary, Mother of God and my Mother,
what light and strength your sweet image
brings me! The most beautiful, the
holiest, the purest of all creatures, so "full
of grace" that you were worthy to bear
within you the Author and Source of all
grace, you do not disdain to give yourself
to me - a poor creature, conscious
of my sin and misery
- as a model of purity,
love and holiness.
          -Divine Intimacy

3 Grateful Gifts for Today:
(So many blessings....take note!)

1. _____
2. _____
3. _____

1 Tiny Tidbit for Today:

(An inspiration, a kind word, a memorable visit with a friend, etc.)

Smile at your family today!

_____
_____
_____

Spiritual Christmas Crib

DEC. 9 – SWADDLING CLOTHES
Prepare these for the Divine Infant by folding
your hands when you pray, and praying slowly
and
thoughtfully.

Jesus, let me love You more and more.

Advent Quote:

What is our personal part in the making of
Christmas? After all, that is the most
important question for us. We cannot do
any other one's part - and no other can do
ours. Some people spend so much time
looking after their neighbor's garden, that
the weeds grow in their own and choke out
the plants and flowers. What about the
little patch of God's great world that is
given to US to tend?
-J.R. Miller

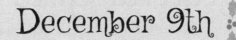

December 9th

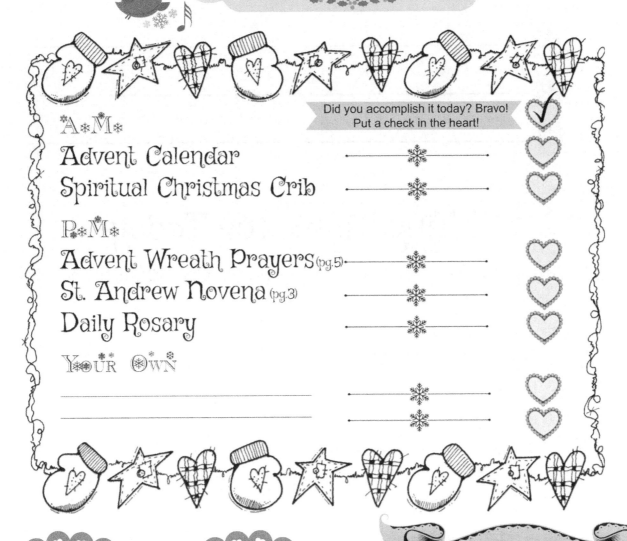

Did you accomplish it today? Bravo!
Put a check in the heart!

A·M·

Advent Calendar

Spiritual Christmas Crib

P·M·

Advent Wreath Prayers (pg. 5)

St. Andrew Novena (pg. 3)

Daily Rosary

Your Own

_____

_____

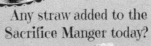

Any straw added to the
Sacrifice Manger today?

The Christmas season is a season of good-will. If we really have in our hearts good-will to men, we shall not only wish everyone well, but we shall seek every opportunity to do good to every one, beginning with those at home. It will make us good wives, good mothers, good neighbors, kind, obliging, ready always to lend a hand, to do another a good turn.
-J.R. Miller

3 Grateful Gifts for Today:
(So many blessings....take note!)

1. _____

2. _____

3. _____

1 Tiny Tidbit for Today:

(An inspiration, a kind word, a memorable visit with a friend, etc.)

Clothe yourself with cheerfulness.

_____

_____

_____

Advent Quote:

Spiritual Christmas Crib

DEC. 10 – BLANKETS
Provide the manger with soft warm blankets. Avoid harsh and angry words; be kind and gentle to all.

Jesus, help me to be meek and humble like You.

This is the season for Advent songs - those age-old hymns of longing and waiting. We found that hardly anybody knows any Advent songs. And we were startled by something else soon after Christmas; Christmas trees and decorations vanish from the shop windows to be replaced by New Year's advertisements.

On our concert trips across the country we also saw that the lighted Christmas trees disappear from homes and front yards and no one thinks to sing a carol as late as January 2nd.

This was all very strange to us, for we were used to the Old-World Christmas, which was altogether different but which we determined to celebrate now in our new country. -Maria von Trapp

December 10th

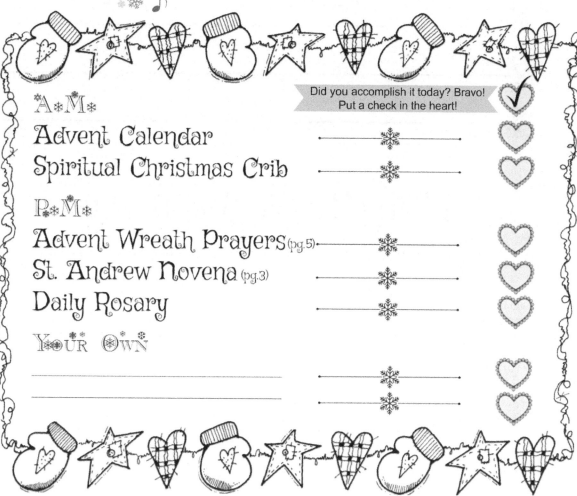

A.M.

Advent Calendar

Spiritual Christmas Crib

Did you accomplish it today? Bravo! Put a check in the heart!

P.M.

Advent Wreath Prayers (pg.5)

St. Andrew Novena (pg.3)

Daily Rosary

Your Own

_____

_____

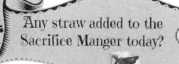

Any straw added to the Sacrifice Manger today?

It is not costly presents at Christmas that are needed; these are only mockeries— if the days between are empty of affectionate expressions.

Jewelry and silks will never atone for the lack of warmth and tenderness. Between husband and wife there should be maintained, without break or pause— the most perfect courtesy, the gentlest attention, the most unselfish amiability, the utmost affectionateness!

J.R. Miller

3 Grateful Gifts for Today:
(So many blessings....take note!)

1. _____

2. _____

3. _____

1 Tiny Tidbit for Today:
(An inspiration, a kind word, a memorable visit with a friend, etc.)

We need to create a home that is joyful and lovely.

_____

_____

_____

Spiritual Christmas Crib

DEC. 11 – FUEL
Bring fuel to the crib of Jesus. Give up your own will; obey your superiors cheerfully and promptly.

Jesus, let me do Your will in all things.

Advent Quote:

On the twelve days of Christmas my True Love sent to me the feast of St. Stephen and the story of King Wenceslaus, the feasts of St. John the Evangelist and the Holy Innocents, the feasts of the Circumcision and the Holy Name of Jesus, and the feast of the Epiphany. And on through the feast of the Holy Family and the commemoration of the Baptism of Christ. If you are loathe to bid farewell to Christmas even then, you may continue it without interruption until Candlemas Day, February 2. However you keep it, long or short, it is a far longer season for the Catholic child than the world understands. –Mary Reed Newland

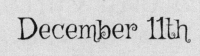

December 11th

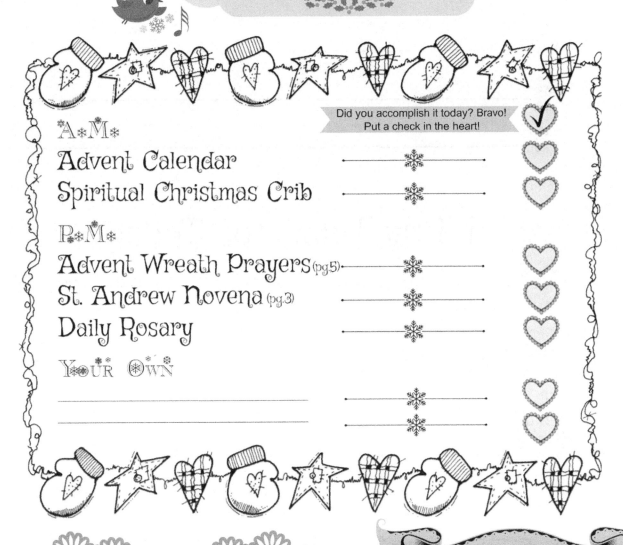

Did you accomplish it today? Bravo!
Put a check in the heart!

A·M·

Advent Calendar

Spiritual Christmas Crib

P·M·

Advent Wreath Prayers (pg.5)

St. Andrew Novena (pg.3)

Daily Rosary

Your Own

_____

_____

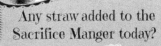

Any straw added to the Sacrifice Manger today?

Thank God for His many blessings. Make the most of each and every day. Enjoy the journey. The world will keep whizzing by but we must take time to smell the roses (or make a snowman). Each day is a gift, each person in your life is special. Take nothing for granted.
–Leane VanderPutten

3 Grateful Gifts for Today:
(So many blessings....take note!)

1. _____

2. _____

3. _____

1 Tiny Tidbit for Today:

(An inspiration, a kind word, a memorable visit with a friend, etc.)

I always find
a way of
being happy.
St. Therese of
Lisieux

_____

_____

_____

Advent Quote:

Spiritual Christmas Crib

DEC. 12 - WATER
Bring fresh, clean water to the crib.
Avoid every untruthful word and
every deceitful act.

**Dearest Mary, obtain for me true
contrition for my sins.**

We must be a maker of Christmas
for others or we cannot make a real
Christmas for ourselves. We need
the sharing of our joy in order to
partake of its real possession. If we
try to keep our Christmas all to
ourselves we will miss half its
sweetness.
J.R. Miller

December 12th
Happy Feast of Our Lady of Guadalupe!

A*M*

Advent Calendar

Spiritual Christmas Crib

Did you accomplish it today? Bravo! Put a check in the heart!

P*M*

Advent Wreath Prayers (pg.5)

St. Andrew Novena (pg.3)

Daily Rosary

Your Own

_____

_____

Any straw added to the Sacrifice Manger today?

"Listen and let it penetrate your heart; do not be troubled or weighed down with grief. Do not fear any illness or vexation, anxiety or pain. Am I not here who am your Mother? Are you not under my shadow and protection? Am I not your fountain of life? Are you not in the folds of my mantle? In the crossing of my arms? Is there anything you need?" (Our Lady's words to her servant, Juan Diego).

3 Grateful Gifts for Today:
(So many blessings....take note!)

1. _____

2. _____

3. _____

1 Tiny Tidbit for Today:

(An inspiration, a kind word, a memorable visit with a friend, etc.)

Laugh and Grow Strong.
-St. Ignatius of Loyola

_____

_____

_____

Advent Quote:

Spiritual Christmas Crib

DEC. 13 – PROVISIONS
Bring a supply of food to the crib. Deprive yourself of some food at mealtime or candy as a treat.

Jesus, be my strength and nourishment.

Either we live the liturgical year with its varying seasons of joy and sorrow, work and rest, or we follow the pattern of the world.
Helen McLoughlin

December 13th
St. Lucy, Pray for us!

Did you accomplish it today? Bravo!
Put a check in the heart!

A*M*
Advent Calendar
Spiritual Christmas Crib

P*M*
Advent Wreath Prayers (pg.5)
St. Andrew Novena (pg.3)
Daily Rosary

Your Own

_____

_____

Any straw added to the
Sacrifice Manger today?

Being a homemaker is one
of the best gifts that we
can bring to our family.
Your joyful presence in the
home is greater than any
present you'll find under
the tree.
-Darlene Schacht

3 Grateful Gifts for Today:
(So many blessings....take note!)

1. _____
2. _____
3. _____

1 Tiny Tidbit for Today:
(An inspiration, a kind word, a memorable visit with a friend, etc.)

Everyone who wants to have progress in the spiritual life needs to have joy.
St. Thomas Aquinas

_____
_____
_____

Advent Quote:

Spiritual Christmas Crib

DEC. 14 – LIGHT
See that the crib has sufficient light. Be neat and orderly about your person; keep everything in its place in your room.

Jesus, be the life and light of my soul.

Children love to anticipate. When there are empty mangers to fill with straw for small sacrifices, when the Mary Candle is a daily reminder on the dinner table, when Advent hymns are sung in the candlelight of a graceful Advent wreath, children are not anxious to celebrate Christmas before the right time. That would offend their sense of honor.
Helen McLoughlin

December 14th

Did you accomplish it today? Bravo!
Put a check in the heart!

*A*M*

Advent Calendar

Spiritual Christmas Crib

*P*M*

Advent Wreath Prayers (pg.5)

St. Andrew Novena (pg.3)

Daily Rosary

Your Own

_____

_____

Any straw added to the Sacrifice Manger today?

"Grant me the privilege of carrying a little Christmas gladness to some who but for me, would go unblessed. Lead me to one, at least, to whom a kindly word will be a blessing. Let me give cheer to one who is discouraged. Give me the privilege of making real to someone, the sweetness and warmth of the love of Christ." -J.R. Miller

3 Grateful Gifts for Today:
(So many blessings....take note!)

1. _____
2. _____
3. _____

1 Tiny Tidbit for Today:
(An inspiration, a kind word, a memorable visit with a friend, etc.)

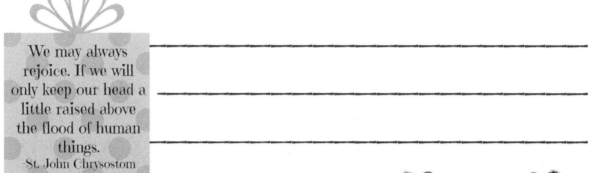

We may always rejoice. If we will only keep our head a little raised above the flood of human things.
-St. John Chrysostom

_____

_____

_____

Spiritual Christmas Crib

DEC. 15 – FIRE
Take care to have the crib of your heart warmed by a cozy fire. Be grateful to God for the love He has shown us in becoming man; behave with grateful respect towards your parents and relatives.

Jesus, how can I return Your love; how can I show my gratitude to You?

Advent Quote:

The Church has traditionally celebrated Christmas for 40 days, culminating on the Feast of the Presentation (Feb. 2).
During this time, the birth of Christ is celebrated as one continuous festival.
It is just as important to celebrate during the Christmas season as it is to prepare for Christ during Advent.
Michaelann Martin

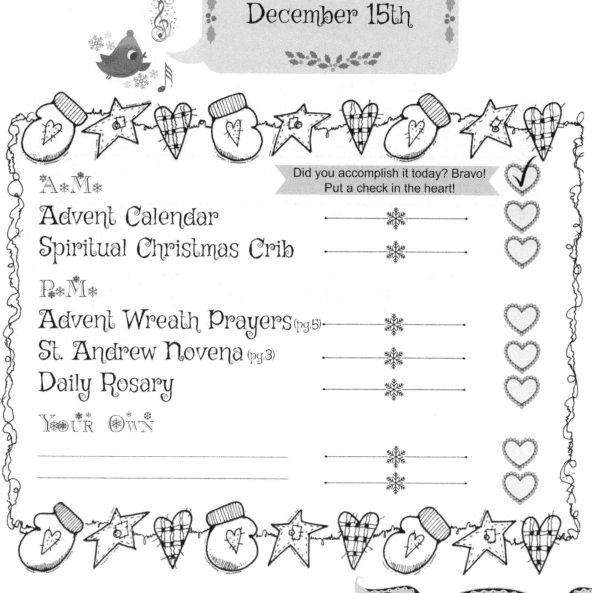

December 15th

A·M·

Advent Calendar

Spiritual Christmas Crib

P·M·

Advent Wreath Prayers (pg.5)

St. Andrew Novena (pg.3)

Daily Rosary

Your Own

_____

_____

Did you accomplish it today? Bravo! Put a check in the heart!

Any straw added to the Sacrifice Manger today?

Every morning we may be tempted to put off our prayers until "later" or skip them altogether because we have much to do and action is where it is at. If we allow the devil to win in the very first struggle of the day, he will win many more of the battles throughout the day. Our Morning Prayers, whether they be said while nursing a baby or changing a diaper, need to be a priority and the very foundation of our daily life.

3 Grateful Gifts for Today:
(So many blessings....take note!)

1. _____

2. _____

3. _____

1 Tiny Tidbit for Today:

(An inspiration, a kind word, a memorable visit with a friend, etc.)

Have patience with all things, but chiefly have patience with yourself.
-St. Francis de Sales

_____

_____

_____

Advent Quote:

Spiritual Christmas Crib

DEC.16 – THE OX

Lead the ox to the crib. Obey cheerfully without making excuses and without asking "why."

I will obey for love of You, Jesus.

Do you want your children to love the Faith? Then inundate them with sweet Catholic traditions! Our Faith then becomes a Living Faith as we celebrate the liturgical year....an ongoing journey that we can grow with as the years go by!

December 16th

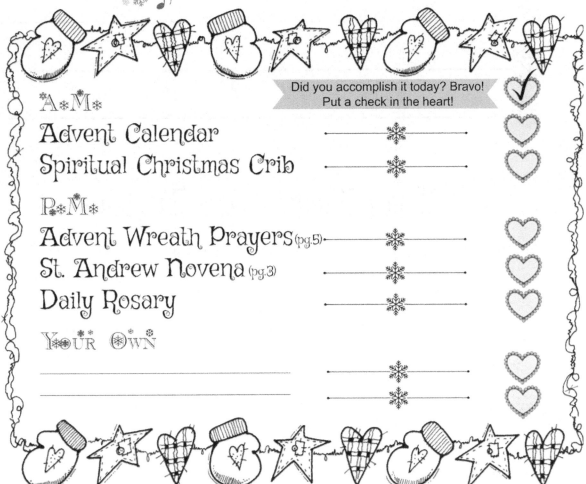

A*M*

Advent Calendar

Spiritual Christmas Crib

P*M*

Advent Wreath Prayers (pg.5)

St. Andrew Novena (pg.3)

Daily Rosary

Your Own

_____

_____

Did you accomplish it today? Bravo!
Put a check in the heart!

We must have a daily habit of prayer; it should be ingrained in us. Morning and Night Prayers, the Rosary and frequent lifting of the mind to God will help us to hear His Voice. The daily habit of prayer leads us to spiritual health. We are more "tuned in" to know what God's will is in our life, to desire it and to do it. By our habit of prayer we will experience the tranquility and happiness that comes from Him Who sees our efforts and loves us so much! He will give us the peace that passeth all understanding....

Any straw added to the Sacrifice Manger today?

3 Grateful Gifts for Today:
(So many blessings....take note!)

1. _____

2. _____

3. _____

1 Tiny Tidbit for Today:

(An inspiration, a kind word, a memorable visit with a friend, etc.)

The Christian should be an alleluia from head to foot.
-St. Augustine

_____

_____

_____

Spiritual Christmas Crib

DEC. 17 – THE DONKEY
Bring the donkey to the crib. Offer to the Divine Infant your bodily strength; use it in the service of others.

Jesus, accept my service of love; I offer it for those who do not love You.

Advent Quote:

It is not strange that all sorts of devotional practices have sprung up around Catholicism, sometimes practices that may seem rather trifling until one realizes that customs cannot be worthless that have evolved from the faith of the people through many hundreds of years, sometimes through well over a thousand years.

-A Candle is Lighted, Stewart Craig

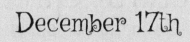

December 17th

Did you accomplish it today? Bravo!
Put a check in the heart!

*A*M*

Advent Calendar

Spiritual Christmas Crib

*P*M*

Advent Wreath Prayers (pg.5)

St. Andrew Novena (pg.3)

Daily Rosary

Your Own

_____

_____

Does your Christmas apron have beautiful stories to tell... Stories of baking and smiling children, setting up Nativity scenes, leading the little ones in their Christmas novenas, lending an ear in spite of a busy household, hospitality mixed with steaming hot chocolate? Our Christmas apron is the symbol of service in this special time of year. 'Tis the Season to be Christlike.
-Leane VanderPutten

Any straw added to the Sacrifice Manger today?

3 Grateful Gifts for Today:
(So many blessings....take note!)

1. _____
2. _____
3. _____

1 Tiny Tidbit for Today:
(An inspiration, a kind word, a memorable visit with a friend, etc.)

_____

Leave sadness to those in the world.
-St. Leonard of Port Maurice

_____

_____

Spiritual Christmas Crib

DEC. 18 – GIFTS
Gather some presents for the Divine Infant and His Blessed Mother. Give alms for the poor and say an extra decade of the rosary.

Come, Jesus, to accept my gifts and to take possession of my heart.

Advent Quote:

When boys and girls drift away from their faith the reason almost always is that this faith has never been a reality to them. The popular celebrations that remained so long in this country did indeed help to make the faith real to those who took part; it could do so again. The parents who enter into these spiritual family customs can give their children treasures, whose value they may not realize until eternity.
-A Candle is Lighted, Stewart Craig

December 18th

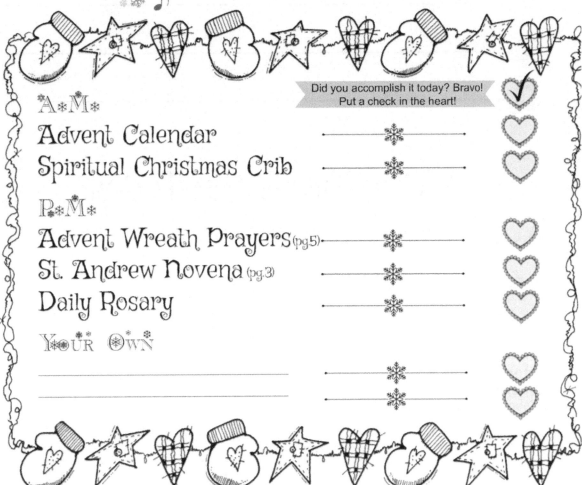

Did you accomplish it today? Bravo!
Put a check in the heart!

A.M.

Advent Calendar

Spiritual Christmas Crib

P.M.

Advent Wreath Prayers (pg.5)

St. Andrew Novena (pg.3)

Daily Rosary

Your Own

_____

_____

Plan on doing the
"Blessing of the Christmas
Tree" this week!
Page 6

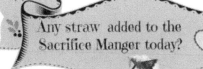

Any straw added to the
Sacrifice Manger today?

Our home is our "Domestic Monastery".
Our monastic bell is each task to which we
are called. We respond immediately, not
because we want to, but because it's time
for that task and time isn't our time, it's
God's time.
-Ron Rolheiser, OMI

3 Grateful Gifts for Today:
(So many blessings....take note!)

1. _____

2. _____

3. _____

1 Tiny Tidbit for Today:

(An inspiration, a kind word, a memorable visit with a friend, etc.)

_____

_____

_____

We who work for God should be light-hearted.
-St. Leonard of Port Maurice

Spiritual Christmas Crib

DEC. 19 – LAMBS
Strive to bring some little lambs, meek and patient. Do not murmur or complain.

Jesus, meek and humble of heart, make my heart like Yours.

Advent Quote:

Don't overwhelm yourself with busy-ness by adding too many pressures to measure up.... DO spend your time on making Advent special and meaningful. Pick a few choice traditions and try to stick to them consistently each year. -Leane Vdp

December 19th

*A*M*

Advent Calendar — ❄ 🤍

Spiritual Christmas Crib — ❄ 🤍

*P*M*

Advent Wreath Prayers (pg.5) — ❄ 🤍

St. Andrew Novena (pg.3) — ❄ 🤍

Daily Rosary — ❄ 🤍

Your Own

_____ ❄ 🤍

_____ ❄ 🤍

Did you accomplish it today? Bravo!
Put a check in the heart!

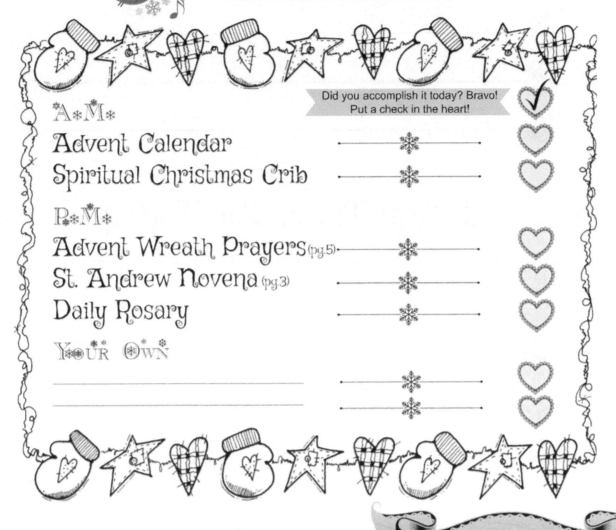

Any straw added to the
Sacrifice Manger today? 🤍

Each day is a chance to grow in virtue and it begins with the little things. Show your husband you care...listen to him, smile at him, give him a hug when he doesn't expect it. Your children are watching and courtesy and love are contagious! Advent can be special...it starts with you!

3 Grateful Gifts for Today:

(So many blessings....take note!)

1. _____

2. _____

3. _____

1 Tiny Tidbit for Today:

(An inspiration, a kind word, a memorable visit with a friend, etc.)

Christian cheerfulness is a modest, hopeful and peaceful joy!

_____

_____

_____

Spiritual Christmas Crib

DEC. 20 – SHEPHERDS

Invite the shepherds to pay homage to our newborn King. Imitate their watchfulness; stress in your speech and thoughts the idea that Christmas is important because Jesus will be born again in you.

Jesus, teach me to love You above all things.

Advent Quote:

Let us continue to add the soft straws of sacrifice and love to the Manger of our Hearts as we prepare for the coming of our Savior. Let us be more attentive to those in our home...where charity begins. "Home is the place where a man should appear at his best." - Fr. Lasance

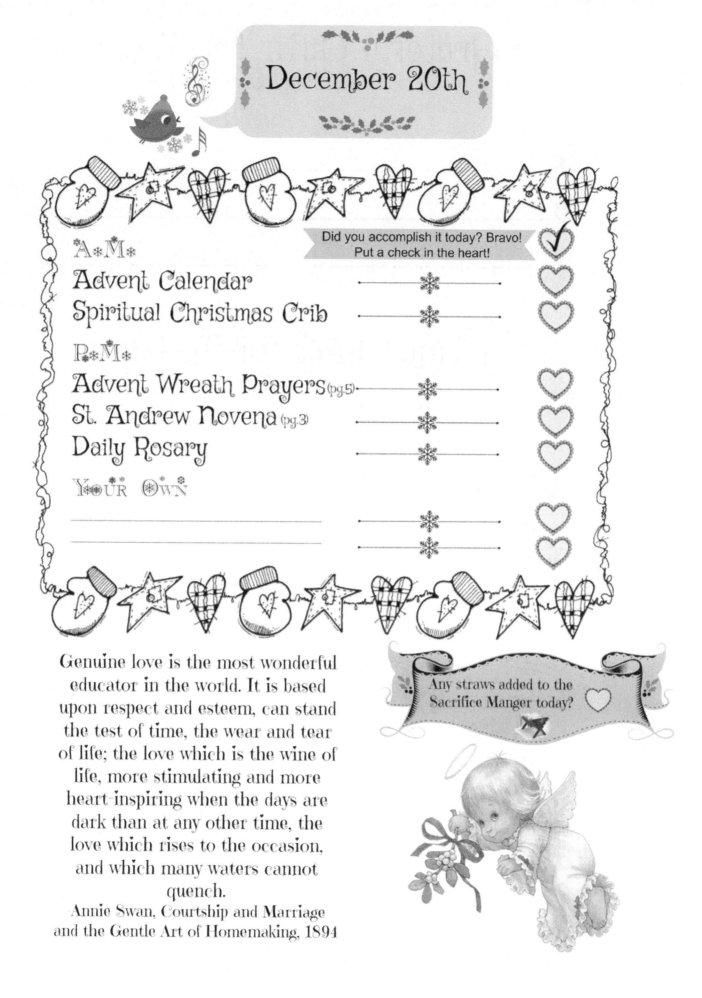

December 20th

A*M*

Advent Calendar ·············· ✳

Spiritual Christmas Crib ·············· ✳

P*M*

Advent Wreath Prayers (pg.5) ·············· ✳

St. Andrew Novena (pg.3) ·············· ✳

Daily Rosary ·············· ✳

Your Own

_____ ·············· ✳

_____ ·············· ✳

Did you accomplish it today? Bravo!
Put a check in the heart!

Genuine love is the most wonderful educator in the world. It is based upon respect and esteem, can stand the test of time, the wear and tear of life; the love which is the wine of life, more stimulating and more heart-inspiring when the days are dark than at any other time, the love which rises to the occasion, and which many waters cannot quench.

Annie Swan, Courtship and Marriage and the Gentle Art of Homemaking, 1894

Any straws added to the Sacrifice Manger today?

3 Grateful Gifts for Today:
(So many blessings....take note!)

1. _____
2. _____
3. _____

1 Tiny Tidbit for Today:

(An inspiration, a kind word, a memorable visit with a friend, etc.)

_____

_____

_____

Often a single word, a friendly smile, is enough to give a depressed or lonely soul fresh life.
-St. Therese of Lisieux

Advent Quote:

Spiritual Christmas Crib

DEC. 21 – THE KEY
Provide the stable with a key to keep out thieves. Exclude from your heart every sinful thought, every rash judgment.

Dear Jesus, close my heart to all that hurts You.

Many traditions connected with observances of Christmas have their origins in Christian, not pagan, culture, despite what we often read. Our heritage of holiday traditions learned from our families which we faithfully continue to practice in our homes for our own children helps to connect both the past and the future. We can make this vital link even stronger when such practices are informed by vigorous faith which most of us also received, by the grace of God, through our families.
-Celebrating Advent and Christmas

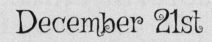

December 21st

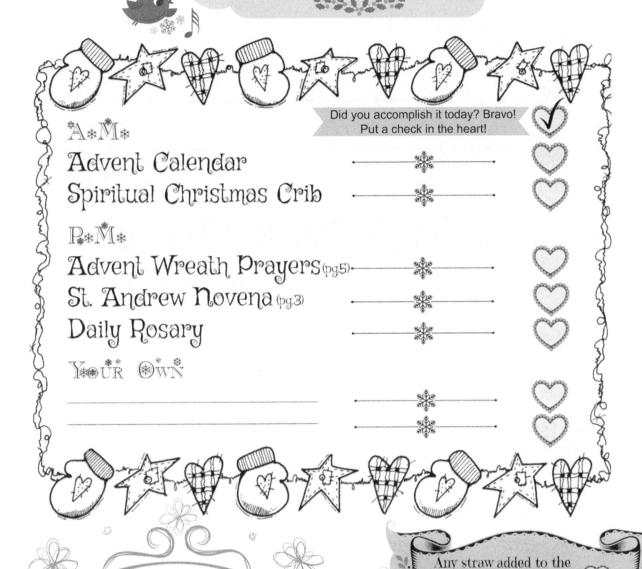

Did you accomplish it today? Bravo! Put a check in the heart!

*A*M*

Advent Calendar

Spiritual Christmas Crib

*P*M*

Advent Wreath Prayers (pg.5)

St. Andrew Novena (pg.3)

Daily Rosary

Your Own

_____

_____

Any straw added to the Sacrifice Manger today?

No other work that God gives any of us to do is so important, so sacred, so far-reaching in its influence, so delicate and easily marred as our homemaking. This is the work of all our life that is most divine. The homemaker works on immortal lives, therefore if we do nothing else well in this world, let us at least build well within our own doors. - J.R. Miller

3 Grateful Gifts for Today:
(So many blessings....take note!)

1. _____
2. _____
3. _____

1 Tiny Tidbit for Today:

(An inspiration, a kind word, a memorable visit with a friend, etc.)

Be merry, really merry. The life of a true Christian should be a perpetual jubilee.
St. Theophone Venard

_____

_____

_____

Spiritual Christmas Crib

DEC. 22 – ANGELS
Invite the angels to adore God with you. Cheerfully obey the inspirations of your Guardian Angel and of your conscience.

Holy Guardian Angel, never let me forget that you are with me always.

Advent Quote:

Joseph turned his eyes away. There was nothing for them but this cave that had lately been a stable; this was their only refuge. Would robbers thrust their rude, dangerous presence into the cave?
Joseph lifted his head in a gesture that expressed hopelessness, desire for something that could not be.
"If only the cave had a door," he said, softly. He turned and enterd the cave, speeding his lagging steps in his anxiety to clear a space for Mary and the expected Child.
- Fr. Daniel A. Lord

December 22nd

A.M.

Advent Calendar

Spiritual Christmas Crib

P.M.

Advent Wreath Prayers (pg.5)

St. Andrew Novena (pg.3)

Daily Rosary

Your Own

Did you accomplish it today? Bravo! Put a check in the heart!

Any straws added to the Sacrifice Manger today?

God will be loved by our children as much as we have permitted Him to be loved. In a strange way, He's at our mercy, and so are they. In His love, He has brought them forth out of us, but He must wait for us to make Him known to them.

Mary Reed Newland

3 Grateful Gifts for Today:
(So many blessings....take note!)

1. _____

2. _____

3. _____

1 Tiny Tidbit for Today:

(An inspiration, a kind word, a memorable visit with a friend, etc.)

_____

_____

_____

Whoever possesses God is happy.
-St. Augustine

Spiritual Christmas Crib

DEC. 23 – ST. JOSEPH
Accompany Saint Joseph from door to door. Learn from him silently and patiently to bear refusals and disappointments. Open wide your heart and beg Our Lord to enter with the Blessed Virgin Mary.

Saint Joseph, help me to prepare for a worthy Christmas Communion.

Advent Quote:

With a yearning that she knew was not hers alone Mary stretched out her arms to embrace a needy world. Then she drew them back to her heart in an embrace that held close and dear the world that was within her, the Word Incarnate.
Joseph appeared at the open mouth of the cave. His face still mirrored his troubled heart.
"I should feel safer for both of you," he said, "if there were a door to this cave."
But Mary smiled at him with all the brave reassurance of her soul.
"I am glad that there is no door," she whispered. And Mary walked into the cave to give the world the God Who was to fling open the doors of heaven, and with a lance open the door of His heart in endless welcome to the weary traveler — man. -Fr. Daniel A. Lord

December 23rd

Did you accomplish it today? Bravo!
Put a check in the heart!

A*M*

Advent Calendar ❄

Spiritual Christmas Crib ❄

P*M*

Advent Wreath Prayers (pg.5) ❄

St. Andrew Novena (pg.3) ❄

Daily Rosary ❄

Your Own

_____ ❄

_____ ❄

Any straw added to the
Sacrifice Manger today?

The many troubles in your household will tend to your edification, if you strive to bear them all in gentleness, patience, and kindness. Keep this ever before you, and remember constantly that God's loving eyes are upon you amid all these little worries and vexations, watching whether you take them as He would desire. Offer up all such occasions to Him, and if sometimes you are put out, and give way to impatience, do not be discouraged, but make haste to regain your lost composure.
-St. Francis de Sales

3 Grateful Gifts for Today:
(So many blessings....take note!)

1. _____

2. _____

3. _____

1 Tiny Tidbit for Today:

(An inspiration, a kind word, a memorable visit with a friend, etc.)

Sweet Jesus, Give joy to my heart!

_____

_____

_____

Spiritual Christmas Crib

DEC.24 – THE BLESSED VIRGIN

Go meet your Blessed Mother. Lead her to the manger of your heart and beg her to lay the Divine Infant in it. Shorten your chats and telephone conversations and spend more time today thinking of Jesus and Mary and Joseph.

Come, dear Jesus, Come; my heart belongs to You.

Advent Quote:

The night of Pagan times was long and dark, and seemed hopeless. Deeper and deeper the nations were sinking in misery and vice. But at length the brightness of the Eternal Light of Heaven, rose, and scattered the darkness, changing the gloom into a brilliant day. So, too, to those who have been long shrouded in the dense gloom of sin or sorrow there waits the same Divine Light ready to scatter their darkness in a moment, if only they will draw nigh to Him. He waits for me, ready to brighten my path, to scatter my sins and sorrows, if I will avail myself of His Love.
-Fr. Richard F. Clarke, S.J.

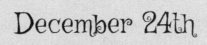

December 24th

Did you accomplish it today? Bravo!
Put a check in the heart!

❋A·M❋

Advent Calendar

Spiritual Christmas Crib

P·M❋

Advent Wreath Prayers (pg.5)

St. Andrew Novena (pg.3)

Daily Rosary

Your Own

_____

_____

It is good sometimes to know that although you have **sacrificed** many of the things modern "emancipated" women value so highly......

your humble position is still the **proudest** in society.

—Fr. Lawrence G. Lovasik

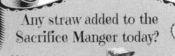

Any straw added to the Sacrifice Manger today?

*Don't forget to put Baby Jesus in His manger!

Over the heads of the patiently watchful shepherds the glory of a star ripped the satin curtains of night. Then angel hands thrust back the torn shreds of gold and purple sky, and the uncontrollable joy of heaven itself leaped forth to sing of a Child.

"Glory to God in the highest," because of that Child. "And on earth peace to men of good will," who from that moment would find themselves kneeling in complete happiness beside that Golden Babe.

Startled, the shepherds looked up at the splendor flung unexpectedly into their drab lives. True peasants, they noted with instinctive relief that their lambs upon the hillside grazed unafraid either of the star, the angel messengers, or the swelling chorus. How could these lambs of the poor (later the favorite subject of the Savior's parables) be flung into confusion by news that the Lamb of God had come to shepherd all His sheep?

"Today is born to you a Savior who is Christ the Lord." Their slow minds were not too dull to realize that tonight their beloved Scriptures were fulfilled. This was the expected King of whom the angels sang. Startling as were the signs by which they were to recognize Him, swaddling clothes and a manger, they broke into headlong flight down the hill and flung themselves in adoration before the Child held up to them by the sweetest mother in all human history.

The childlike faith and hope of simple peasants found fulfillment in a Child. Christmas came rushing into their eventless lives on the wings of an Infant's smile, and the low-voiced gratitude of a mother welcoming these first Christmas guests who, in a beautiful single gesture, adored her Son and filled her day with the sweet fragrance of their Christmas greeting.
-Father Daniel A. Lord

"For Christmas begins and ends with a Child...."
Fr. Daniel A. Lord

May the joy of Christmas reign in our hearts all through the year!

-ↈ· Merry Christmas! ·ↇ-

About the Author

Mrs. Leane VanderPutten lives in rural Kansas with her husband of over 30 years.

She is the mother and grandmother of 11 children and 23 grandchildren....and growing.

They are devoted to Tradition within the Fold of the Catholic Church, homeschoolers with 5 children still at home.

Their family life is lively, full of faith and joy!

Made in the USA
Monee, IL
17 December 2020